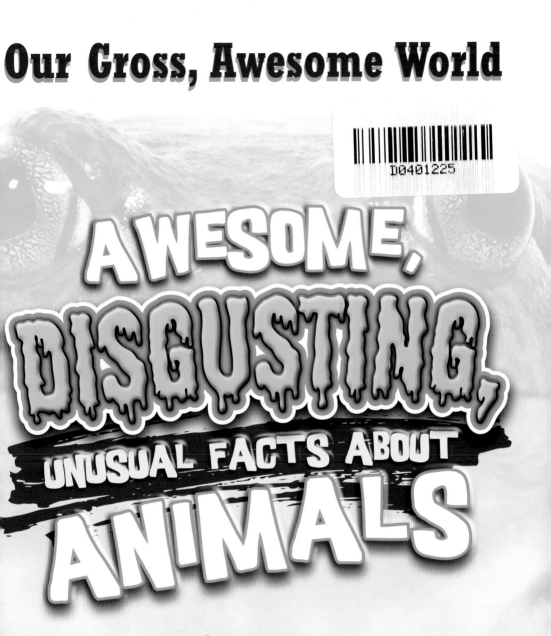

Our Gross, Awesome World

D0401225

AWESOME, DISGUSTING, UNUSUAL FACTS ABOUT ANIMALS

Eric Braun

BLACK
RABBIT
BOOKS

Hi Jinx is published by Black Rabbit Books
P.O. Box 3263, Mankato, Minnesota, 56002.
www.blackrabbitbooks.com
Copyright © 2019 Black Rabbit Books

Marysa Storm, editor; Michael Sellner, designer;
Catherine Cates, production designer;
Omay Ayres, photo researcher

Library of Congress Cataloging-in-Publication Data
Names: Braun, Eric, 1971- author.
Title: Awesome, disgusting, unusual facts about
animals / by Eric Braun.
Description: Mankato, Minnesota : Black Rabbit Books,
[2019] | Series: Hi jinx. Our gross, awesome world |
Audience: Ages 9-12. | Audience: Grades 4 to 6. |
Includes bibliographical references and index.
Identifiers: LCCN 2017044820 (print) | LCCN 2017054814
(ebook) | ISBN 9781680726152 (e-book) | ISBN
9781680726091 (library binding) | ISBN 9781680727517
(paperback) | ISBN 9781644663042 (paperback)
Subjects: LCSH: Animals–Miscellanea–Juvenile literature. |
Children's questions and answers.
Classification: LCC QH48 (ebook) | LCC QH48 .B8245 2018
(print) | DDC 590.2–dc23
LC record available at https://lccn.loc.gov/2017044820

Image Credits

Alamy: Anton Sorokin, 23 (bttm); BIOSPHOTO, Cover (spider), 10–11
(spider); blickwinkel, 18 (bttm); dpa picture archive, 18 (badger); Erik
Grønningsæter, 8 (bkgd); Natural Visions, 11 (toad); Nigel Cattlin, 16
(top bug); en.wikipedia.org: Muhammad Mahdi Karim, 13 (beetle);
iStock: CandO_Designs, 7 (ill. koala); npr.org: National Public Radio, 16
(ant); Science Source: Anthony Bannister, 20 (bats); Eye of Science, 16 (btm
beetle); Shutterstock: Angeliki Vel, 19 (sun), 20 (arrow); anna lopatina, 21
(bkgd); Apple's Eyes Studio, 7 (photo); anfisa focusova, 16 (bkgd); blambca,
19 (vomit); Christos Georghiou, 4 (torn paper); Fotana, 18 (torn paper);
frescomovie, 7 (paper); Fredrik Stenström, 10 (sifaka); JonathanC Photography,
12–13 (cheetah); Kobzev Dmitry, 15 (mucus texture); Konstantin G, 14 (flying
fish); lady-luck, 19 (skunk); Lana Langlois, 1 (bkgd), 14–15 (frog); Loradora, 18
(bees); Lucasdm, 3; Memo Angeles, 13 (rabbit); mire, 19 (bkgd); opicobello, 9 (torn
paper); Pasko Maksim, Back Cover (top), 12 (bttm), 23 (top), 24 (top); picturepartners,
8 (pellet); Pitju, 21 (curled paper); Ron Dale, Cover (marker stroke), 1 (marker stroke),
3 (marker stroke), 5 (marker stroke), 6, 10 (marker stroke), 14 (top marker stroke), 20
(marker stroke); Sarawut Padungkwan, 9 (bttm), 15 (snakes); 16 (ill. bug); schwarzhana, 4
(fork, knife); Tony Campbell, 19 (vulture); totallypic, 14 (arrow); Trahcus, 2–3, 9 (top); TTL
media, 4 (octopus); Tueris, 14 (marker strokes); VectorShots, 4 (shrimp), 5 (crab); Vector
Tradition SM, 4 (octopus eyes); vixenkristy, 7 (poo); Yellow Cat, 21 (tentacle); your, 12
(clouds) Every effort has been made to contact copyright holders for material reproduced
in this book. Any omissions will be rectified in subsequent printings if notice is given to
the publisher.

CONTENTS

4

Chapter 1
HOW AWESOME, DISGUSTING, AND UNUSUAL ARE ANIMALS?

Ever heard of an animal that eats itself? Or one that makes itself explode? How about a fish that flies?

Animals can be disgusting and unusual. Get ready to be surprised by the amazing things animals do. (You might get a little grossed out too!)

Chapter 2

THEY REALLY EAT THAT?

When octopuses are healthy, they eat crabs and shrimp. But when they are sick, crazy things happen. Sometimes octopuses eat their own arms! They eat their arms because of **stress** or a **virus**.

Adult koalas eat poisonous leaves. Baby koalas can't eat them. To help, their mothers feed them pap. Basically, pap is poop. It has **bacteria** that help the babies **digest** the leaves. Without pap, baby koalas could die.

You can find feathers, fur, bones, and claws in owl pellets.

Talk about a Mouthful!

Owls eat animals whole. Later, they spit up small pellets. The pellets include all the animal parts they couldn't digest.

Snakes eat their food whole too. And they can eat a lot! Snakes often eat animals 75 to 100 percent of their own size.

Chapter 3

TIME TO GET MOVING

Sifakas have long legs and short arms. They're made to jump from tree to tree. When sifakas travel on the ground, they leap using their legs. They use outstretched arms and tails for balance. These animals look like they're surfing or dancing.

To attract mates, male peacock
spiders dance. They throw their arms
into the air. They scurry back and
forth, showing off their colors.
Talk about putting on a show!

Female Suriname
toads carry their eggs
beneath their back
skin. When the eggs
hatch, baby toads
climb out of their
mothers' **flesh**.

Running fast puts a lot of stress on cheetahs' bodies. Cheetahs can get brain damage if they run too fast for

Freaky Fast

Cheetahs are the fastest land animals. These cats can **sprint** up to 70 miles (113 kilometers) per hour.

What's the world's fastest insect? That's the Australian tiger beetle. These bugs can run about 5.6 miles (9 km) per hour. But their visual systems aren't strong enough to keep up. At top speeds, the bugs are blind. They have to slow down to see.

Chapter 4
ATTACKING AND DEFENDING

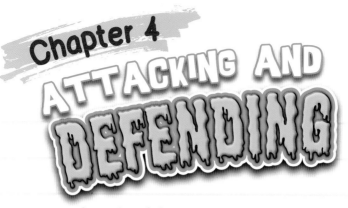

One kind of fish escapes **predators** by flying. Flying fish swim about 37 miles (60 km) per hour. Then they launch out of the water. Their fins act like wings. They glide more than 600 feet (183 meters).

Tomato frogs are bright red. Their color warns other animals not to eat them. If animals do attack, the frogs' skin makes a sticky **mucus**. It makes their enemies' lips stick together.

cereal leaf beetle

exploding ant

bombardier beetle

Brutal Bugs

Bugs have gross and unusual ways of protecting themselves.

Young cereal leaf beetles stay safe by smearing poop over their bodies. Most predators don't want poopy food. The poop may also act as **camouflage**.

One kind of ant defends its space by blowing itself up. That's right! These insects make themselves explode. A poisonous yellow goo spreads all over the enemies.

Bombardier beetles squirt boiling **chemicals** at predators. Ouch! A chemical reaction inside the beetles' bodies makes this defense possible.

Badgers, Newts, and Vultures

Honey badgers aren't Africa's biggest animal. But they are one of its fiercest. These animals take on killer bees to get honey. They will even eat venomous snakes.

A Spanish ribbed newt uses its own ribs as protection. When attacked, it pushes its ribs out. The sharp ribs break through the skin. They help defend the newt.

Some vultures have an interesting way of defending themselves. When threatened, they throw up. The vomit's smell drives away predators.

Chapter 5

GET IN ON THE HI JINX

Animals do many amazing things. Some scientists studied Egyptian bats. They wanted to know what the bats communicated about. So they made a computer program. It matched the bats' noises with their actions.

And guess what they were doing. They were yelling at each other! The bats were arguing and complaining. They yelled about food, sleeping spots, **mating**, and space.

Take It One Step More

1. Do you think other animals "complain" about the same things as bats? Why or why not?

2. Some vultures throw up to protect themselves. How might that be similar to when you get sick? How is it different?

3. Which fact surprised you the most? Why did it surprise you?

GLOSSARY

bacteria (bak-TEER-ee-uh)—a small living thing

camouflage (KA-muh-flazh)—something, such as color or shape, that protects an animal from attack by making the animal difficult to see in the area around it

chemical (KEH-muh-kuhl)—a substance that can cause a change in another substance

digest (DY-jest)—to change the food eaten into a form that can be used by the body

flesh (FLESH)—the soft parts of the body of an animal or person

mate (MAYT)—to join together to produce young

mucus (MYOO-kuhs)—a thick liquid that is produced in some parts of the body

predator (PRED-uh-tuhr)—an animal that eats other animals

sprint (SPRINT)—a short run at top speed

stress (STRES)—something that causes strong feelings of worry or anxiety

virus (VAHY-ruhs)—a tiny organism that causes a disease

BOOKS

Chigna, Charles. *Animal Planet Strange Unusual Gross and Cool Animals.* New York: Time Inc. Books, 2016.

Perish, Patrick. *Disgusting Animals.* Totally Disgusting. Minneapolis: Bellwether Media, 2014.

Weird but True: Animals. Weird but True. Washington, D.C.: National Geographic Kids, 2018.

WEBSITES

13 Facts to Gross Out Your Parents
kids.nationalgeographic.com/explore/ 13-facts-to-gross-out-your-parents/

Fun Animal Facts for Kids
www.sciencekids.co.nz/sciencefacts/animals.html

Top 10 Animal Gross-Outs
www.animalplanet.com/wild-animals/ 10-animal-gross-outs/

INDEX

A

amphibians, 11, 15, 18

B

bats, 20

birds, 8, 9, 19

C

cheetahs, 12, 13

F

flying fish, 5, 14

H

honey badgers, 18

I

insects, 5, 13, 17

K

koalas, 6

O

octopuses, 5, 6

P

peacock spiders, 11

S

sifakas, 10

snakes, 9